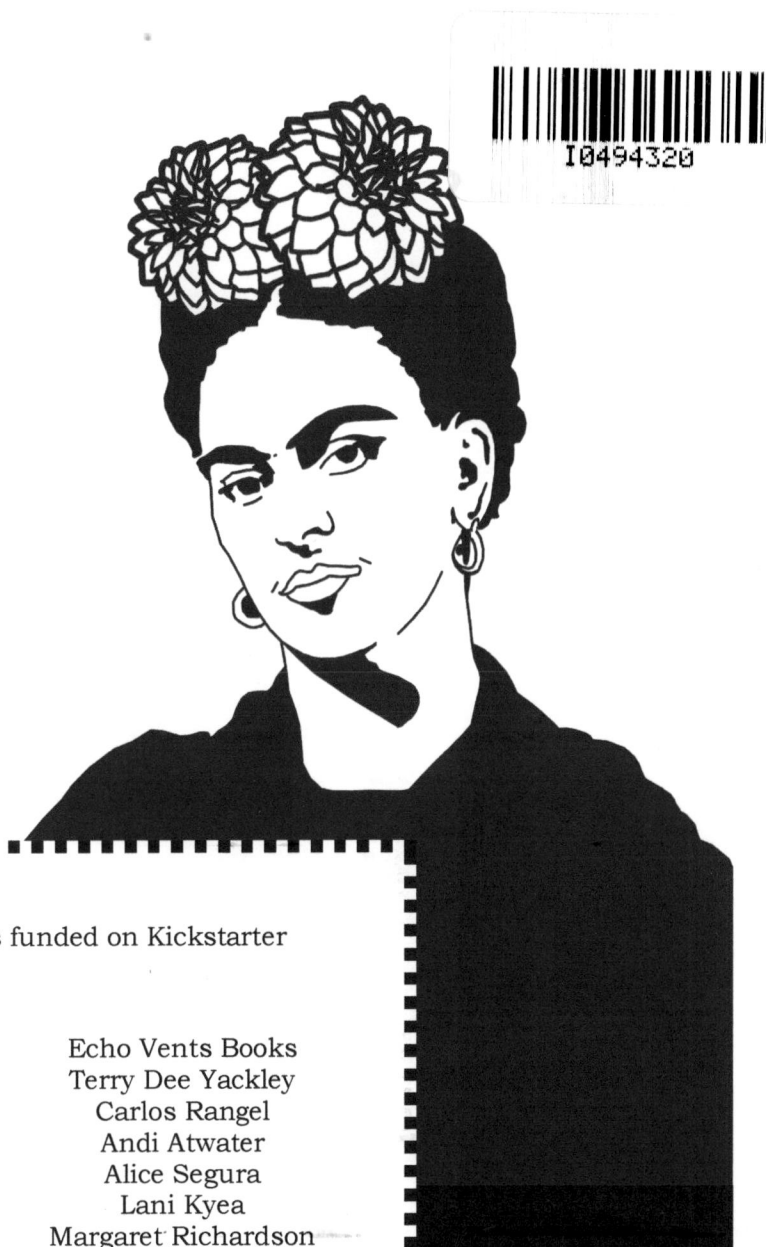

This issue of Bad Influence was funded on Kickstarter by these brave backers:

Marti Keller
Anna Maguire
Arlene Taylor
Cindy Blood
Carolyn Myles
Mary Salerno
Valerie Thomas
Fonda Rush
Esta Beerman-Price
Amy O'Brien
Vicki Jacobs
Patricia Hendricks
Julia Simonello
Laura Rajsic-Lanier
Sharnie Riley
Kate Bakker
Suzan de Lison
Vicki Hawes
Lynda Underwood

Echo Vents Books
Terry Dee Yackley
Carlos Rangel
Andi Atwater
Alice Segura
Lani Kyea
Margaret Richardson
Eugene Villarreal
Louise Foster
Fran Tuttle
Diane Redmer Moore
Angela Zacharek
Mary Pendergrass
LA Smith
JM
Cindy Couling
Jill Minehart
Elly Vitullo
Maya Jansen - Beijn

Thanks so much for making it happen!

I0494320

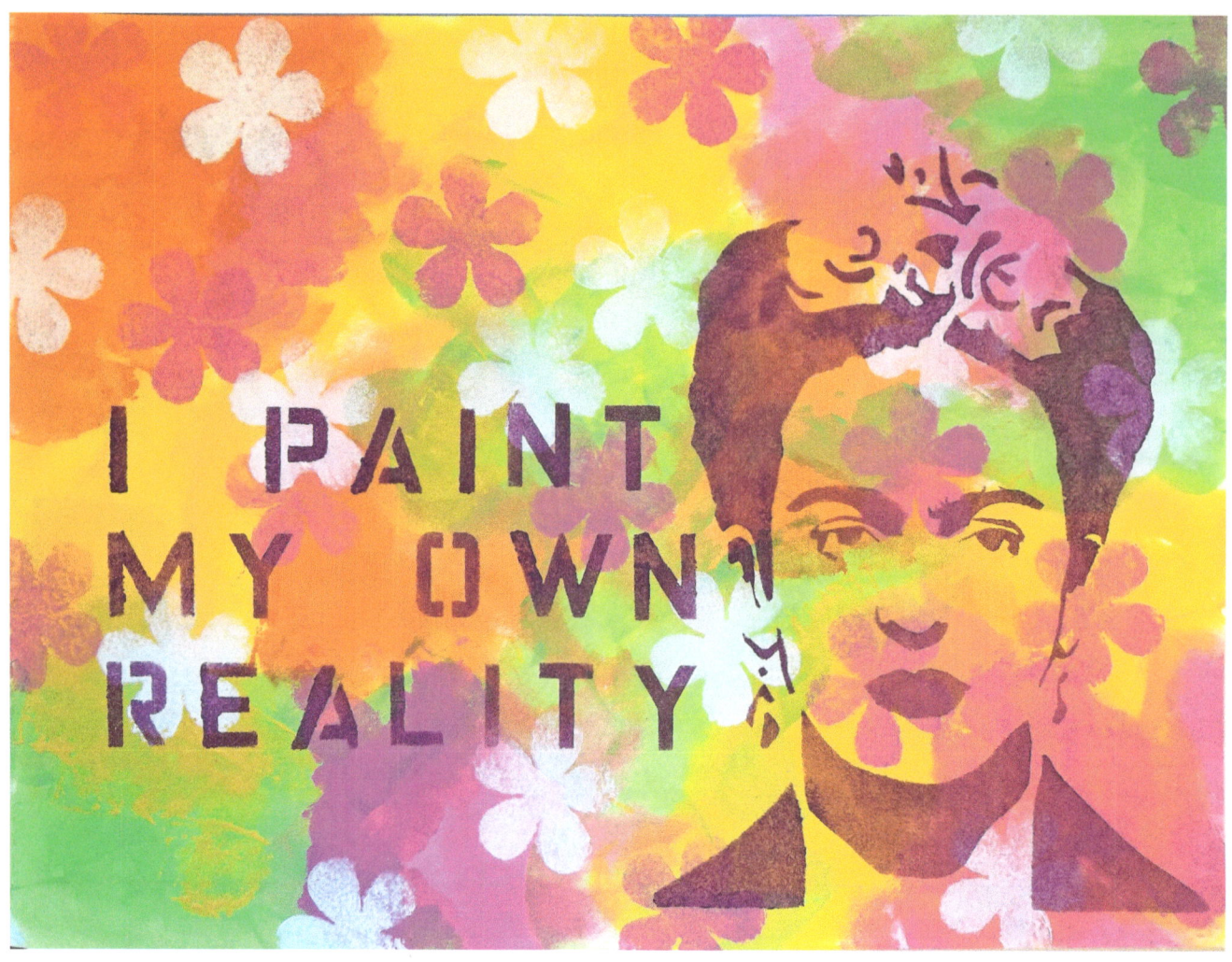

A Few Words From Lisa

It's been a year since the last issue of Bad Influence, and this one happened purely on the basis of a sudden spark, much like the Day of the Dead issue did three years ago.

The idea popped into my head out of nowhere: how have I never done a project centered on Frida Kahlo? There's nary an altered book, art journal, artist trading card swap, or deco exchange in my long and checkered list of collaborative art projects that has been inspired by Frida. How is that possible? Because, let's be honest: Frida's image, and her work, have been endlessly used by many artists, even though most of her paintings and photos remain under legal protection.

So, here's the Inspired by Frida issue, packed with artwork and postcards from over a dozen brave artists who took up the challenge to create original pieces that are inspired by her work, while not appropriating any of it. I also asked each artist to share their thoughts on why Frida inspires them, and have included those in this issue.

I hope you are as Inspired by Frida as we are...

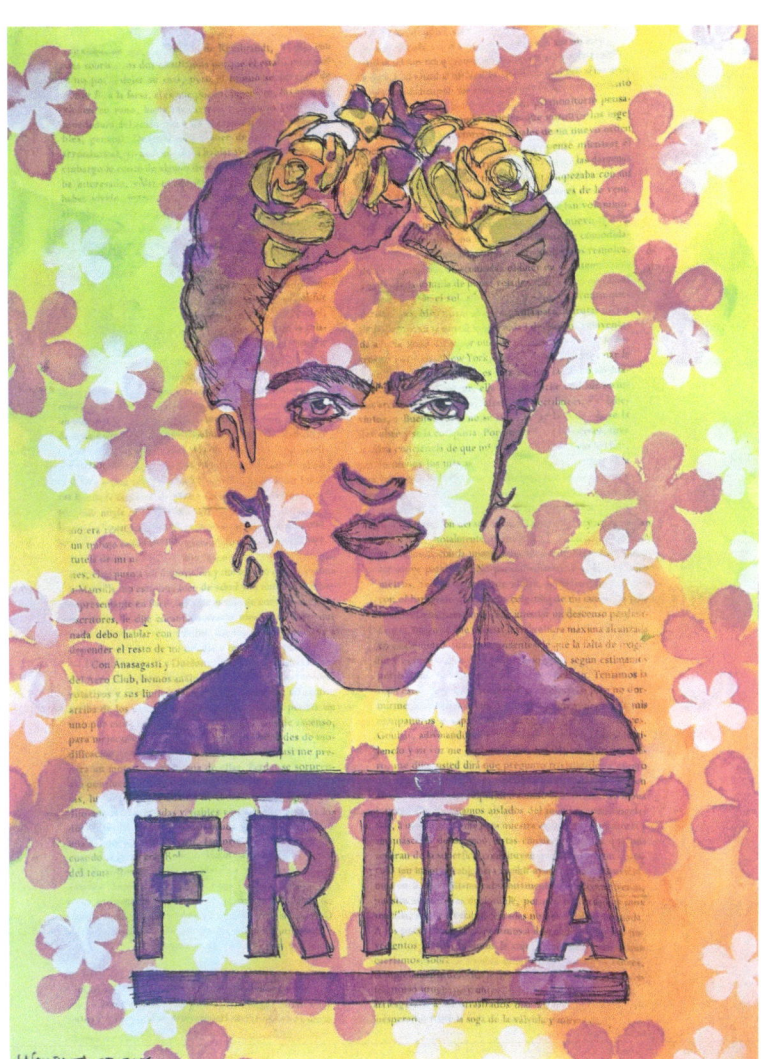

Above: *Frida*
Stenciled acrylics and pen on 11 x 15 inch watercolor paper.

Left: *I Paint My Own Reality*
Stenciled acrylics on 11 x 15 inch watercolor paper.

A Brief Biography of Frida Kahlo

Frida Kahlo was born Magdalena Carmen Frieda Kahlo y Calderon in Coyoacan, Mexico, July 6th, 1907, to a Hungarian-Jewish father, and a mother of Spanish and Mexican Indian descent. Her father, Willhelm, was the son of a jeweler, and emigrated to Mexico at the age of 19, changing his name to Guillermo, and trading is Jewish faith for atheism. He married Frida's mother, Mathilde, and learned the photography trade from her father, eventually becoming a professional photographer himself.

Frida was stricken with polio at age 6, leaving her right leg deformed, and the growth of her right foot stunted. She was teased by her classmates at the Colegio Aleman, Mexico's German school, despite her attempts to hide her hide her deformed leg under long skirts and pants.

In 1922, Frida enrolled at the Escuela National Preparatoria school, where she planned to study medicine. Attending prestigious school, located in Mexico City, required Frida to ride a bus an hour to and from her home in Coyoacan. In 1925, in her senior year at the school, her bus was hit by a a trolley car. Frida sustained multiple injuries; a shattered pelvic bone, fractures of her spine, collarbone, and ribs and other severe injuries. Doctors to doubted that she would survive, and over the course of her life, she endured over 30 operations, and was in almost constant pain, due to these injuries.

During the year she spent convalescing after the accident, Frida began to paint. Her

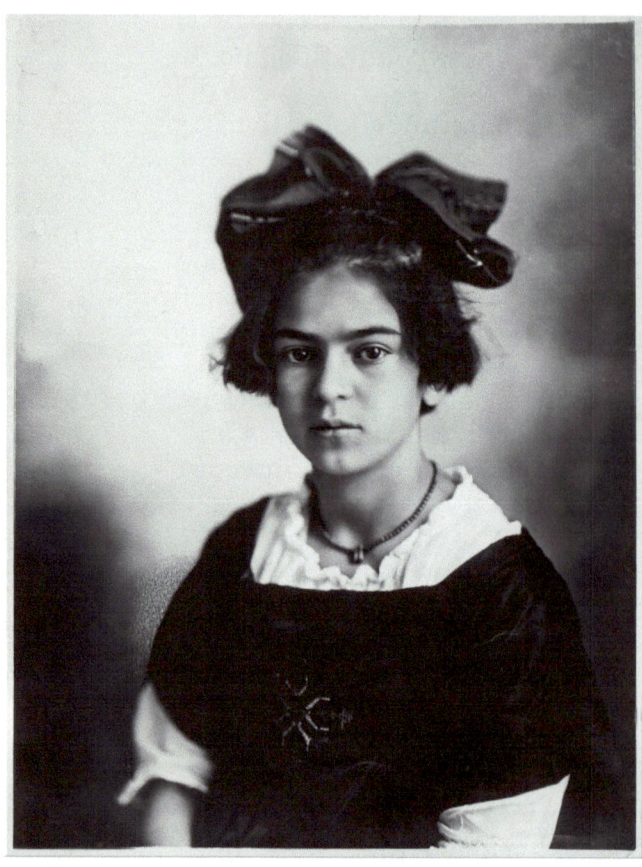

Photo of Frida at age 11, taken in 1919 by her father, Guillermo Kahlo. Courtesy of Wikimedia Commons.

father gave her a set of paints and brushes, and her mother had an easel built that could sit on the bed. They hung a mirror from her canopy, so she could see herself, and she began painting self-portraits. She had little formal training, and her paintings were deliberately naïve, and filled with the colors and forms of Mexican folk art.

By 1927, Frida's health had improved enough that she was once more living a more normal life. She resumed contact with some of her school friends, and joined the

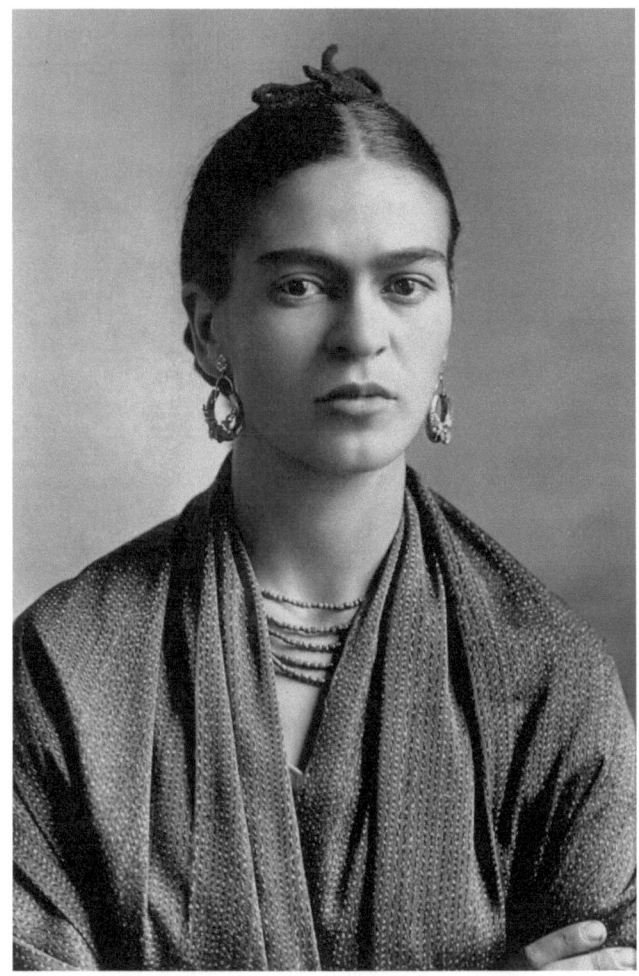

Photo of Frida in 1932, taken by Guillermo Kahlo. Courtesy of Wikimedia Commons.

remarriage, her poor health, and several miscarriages ending in her inability to bear a child. During her lifetime, she produced 151 paintings, many of which chronicle both the emotional turmoil of these events, and her increasing physical pain. 55 of her paintings are self-portraits.

A year before her death in 1953, after successful exhibits abroad, Frida finally had her first solo exhibition in Mexico. She died at the age of 47, in 1954, and at her request, she was cremated. At the crematorium, as mourners stood at the open doors, the heat from the flames caused her body to suddenly sit upright, her hair ablaze. In her final journal entry, she wrote, "I hope the end is joyful, and I hope never to return."

Young Communist League. Through these friends, she met artist Diego Rivera, at a party in 1928. Rivera was 20 years her senior, and already quite well-known. Soon after they met, Frida showed Diego her paintings, and asked for his opinion. He told her she had talent, and encouraged her to keep painting. He began to court Frida, and during their courtship, suggested she wear traditional Mexican clothing. Diego and Frida married in a civil ceremony in 1929.

Frida's marriage to Diego was stormy, and survived many infidelities on both sides, the pressures of diverging careers, divorce,

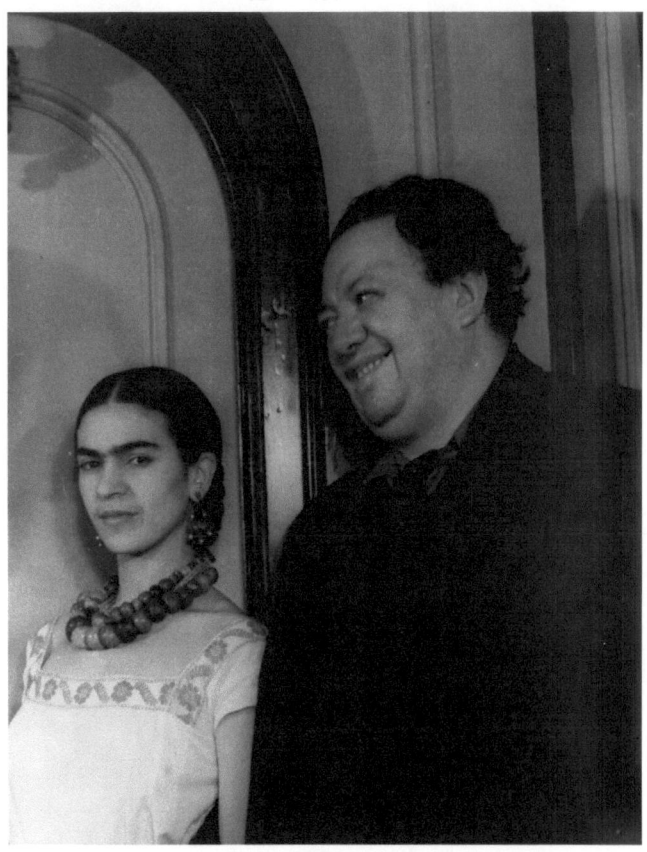

Portrait of Frida Kahlo and Diego Rivera, 1932. Courtesy of the Carl Van Vechten Photographs collection at the Library of Congress.

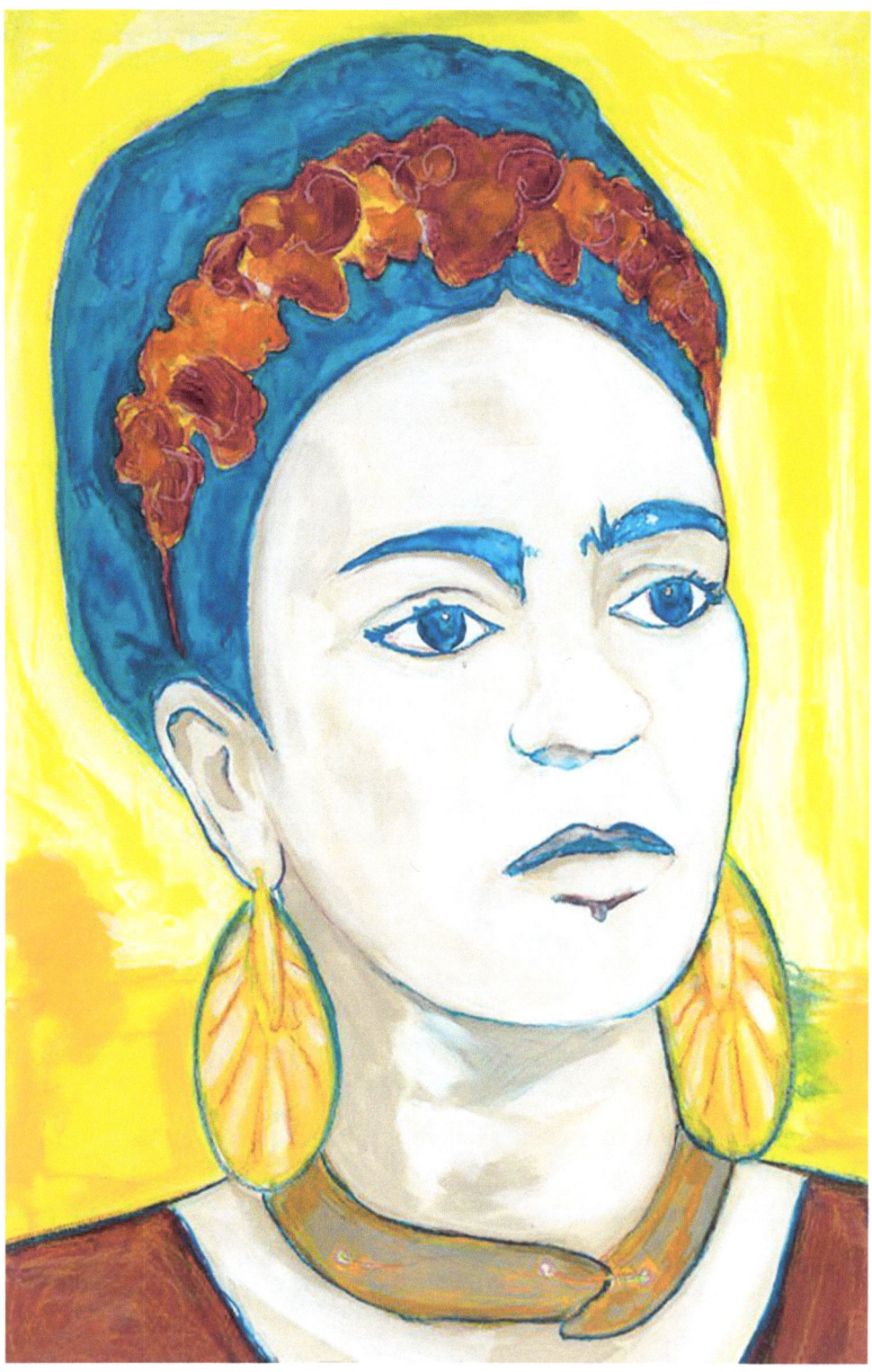

Here's what Allegra had to say about Frida:

"I was born and raised in Latin America, so I identify with Frida as an artist. Ironically, I did not hear about her until I moved to the United States."

More of Allegra's work can be seen on her Instagram account, allegra.sleep.

Frida
Acrylics and water media on 24 x36 inch hardboard.

Allegra Sleep

Taos, New Mexico

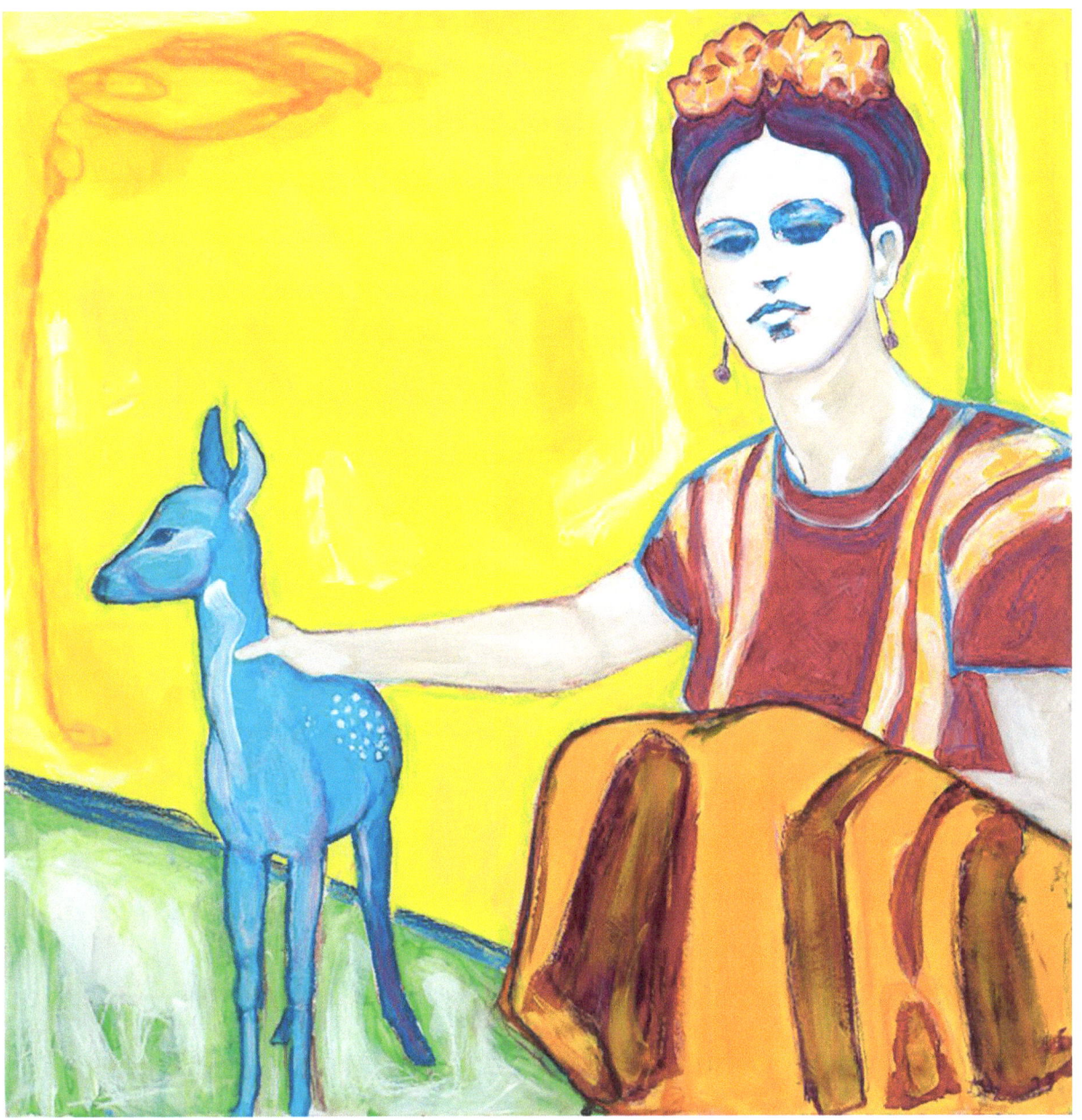

Frida and Fawn
Acrylics and water media on 30 x30 inch hardboard.

Cindy Couling

East Providence, Rhode Island

Here's what Cindy had to say about Frida:

"She wasn't afraid to put her emotions on the canvas and worry what people thought about them. She inspires me to try to create work that isn't just 'safe'."

More of Cindy's work can be seen on her web site, couling.com.

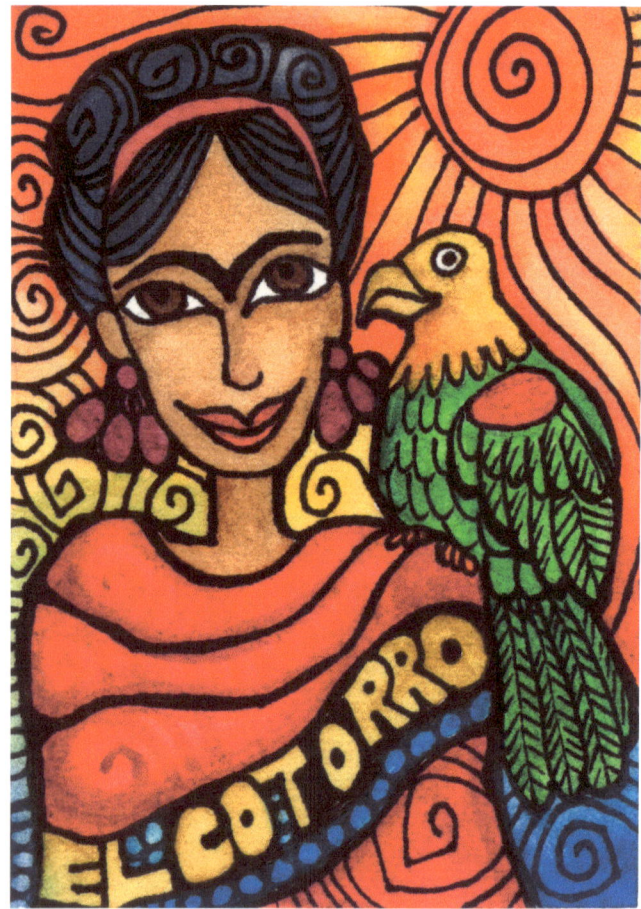

El Cotorro (The Parrot) Loteria
Watercolor and ink on 5 x 7 inch watercolor paper.

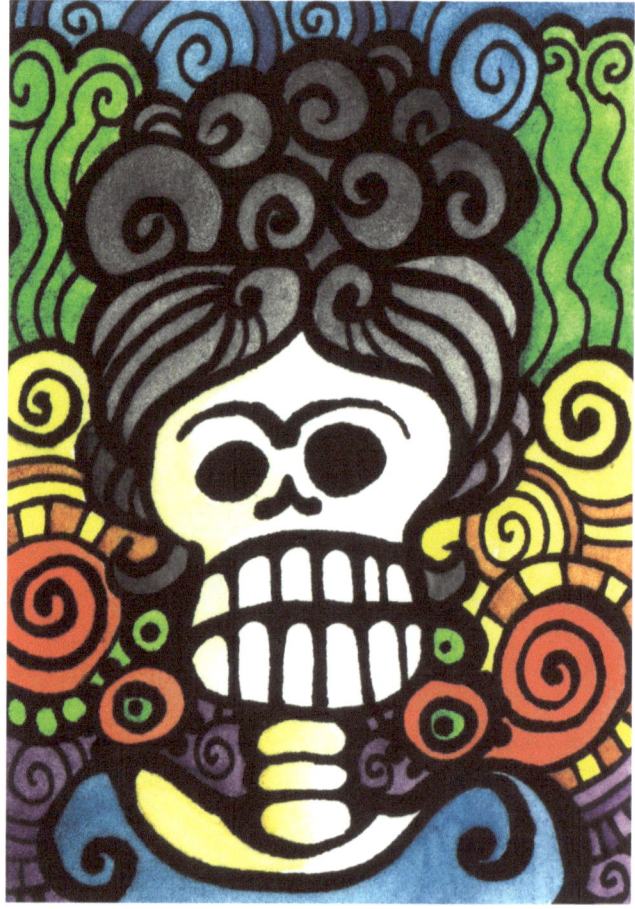

La Frida Catrina
Watercolor and ink on 5 x 7 inch watercolor paper.

Jennifer Gillooly Cahoon

East Providence, Rhode Island

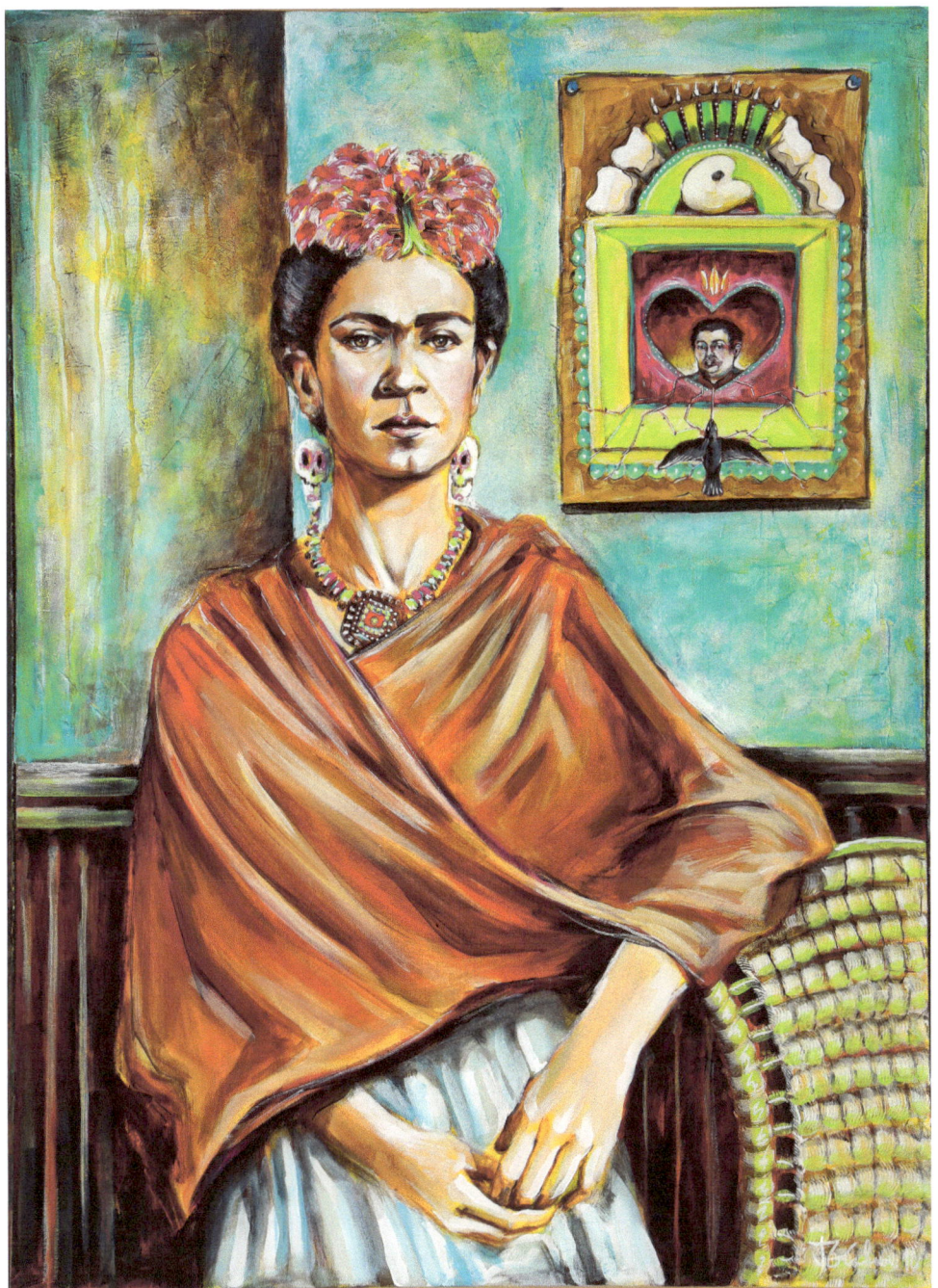

Here's what Jennifer had to say about Frida:

"Like many other female artists, I consider Frida to be my patron goddess of art. I find the way she created art and lived her life in the most genuine, raw, unapologetic way possible to be incredibly inspiring. Despite chronic pain and monumental struggles, she never ceased to express her true self on canvas."

More of Jennifer's work can be seen on her web site, jgcahoon.com.

Frida's Sacred Heart
Acrylic paint on 30 x 40 x 2 inch gallery wrapped canvas.

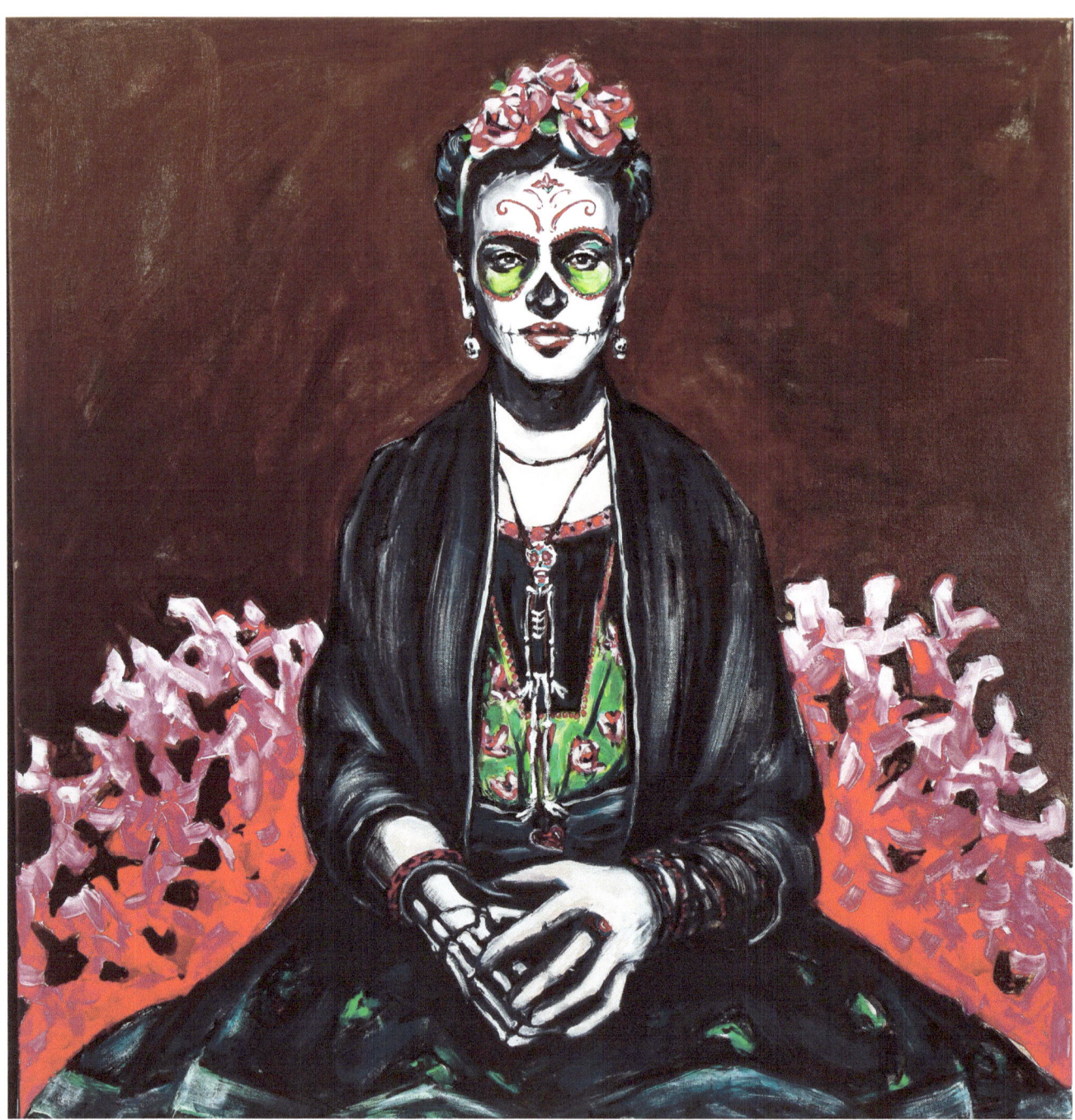

Above: *Frida Kahlo Seated, Dia de Los Muertos*
Mixed media on 36 x 36 x 1 inch canvas.

Right: *Frida Kahlo in Purple, Dia de Los Muertos*
Water miscible oil paint on 24 x 36 x 2 inch gallery wrapped canvas.

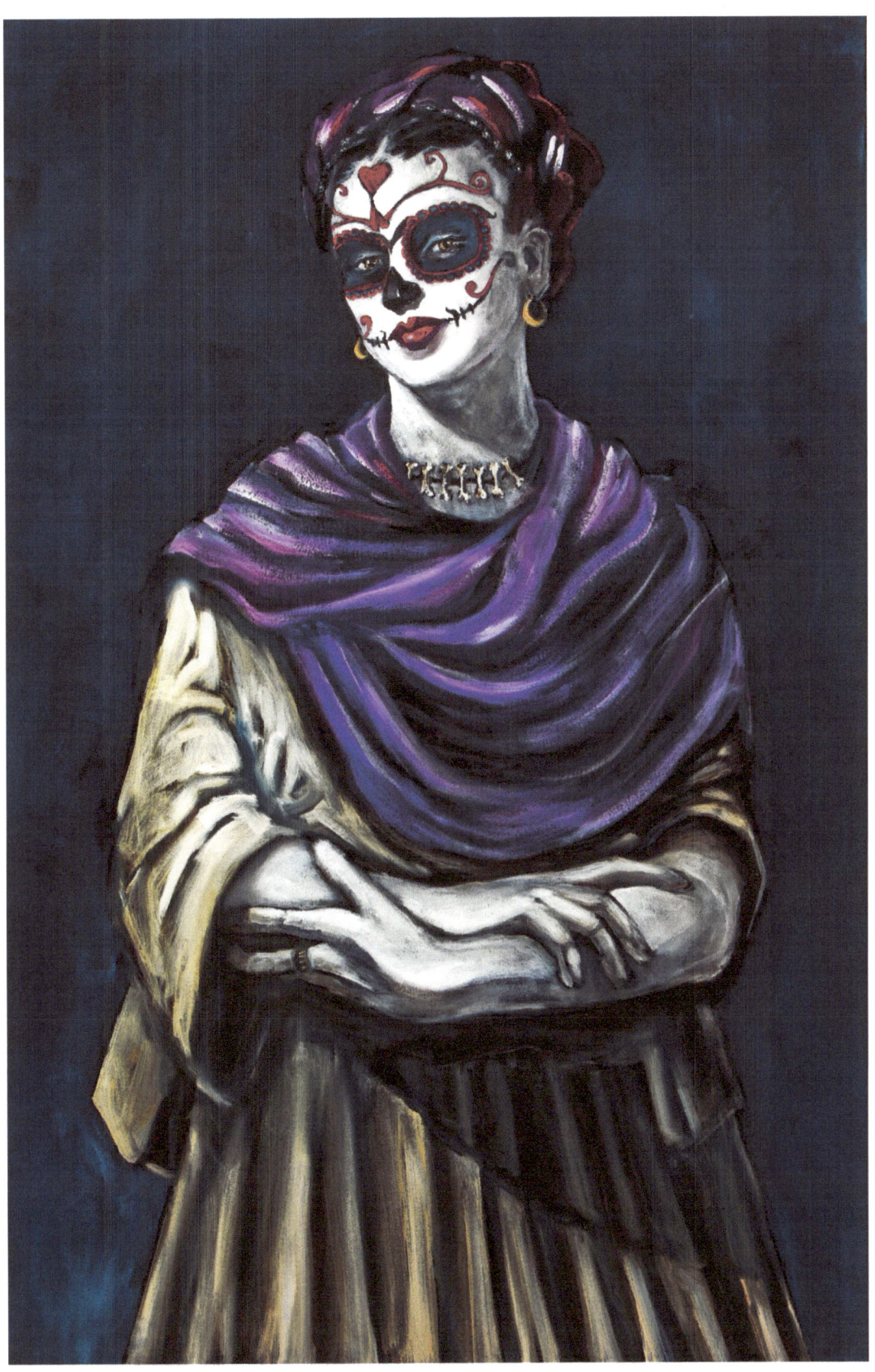

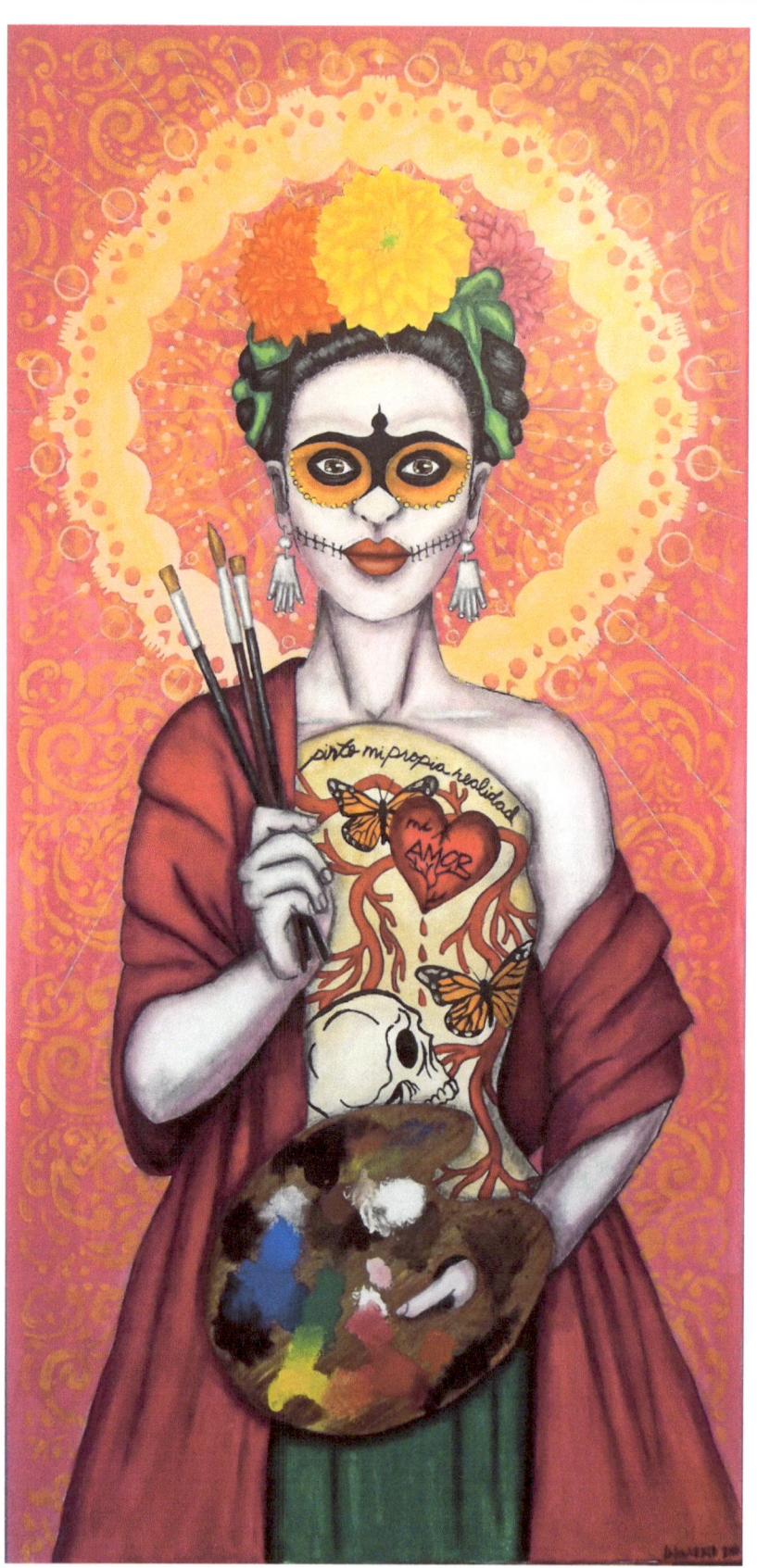

Left: *La Patrona (The Patron Saint)* Mixed media on 24 x 48 inch canvas.

"So much art training focuses on learning to paint what we see. Frida's work inspires me because she painted what she felt. Her paintings let you experience the pain, heartache, and anguish she experienced in her life. That ability to just let the pain flow out onto the canvas is something to which I aspire."

More of my work can be seen at LisaVollrath.com and TenTwoStudios.com.

Right: *La Pintora (The Painter)* Mixed media on 18 x 24 inch canvas.

Lisa Vollrath

Euless, Texas

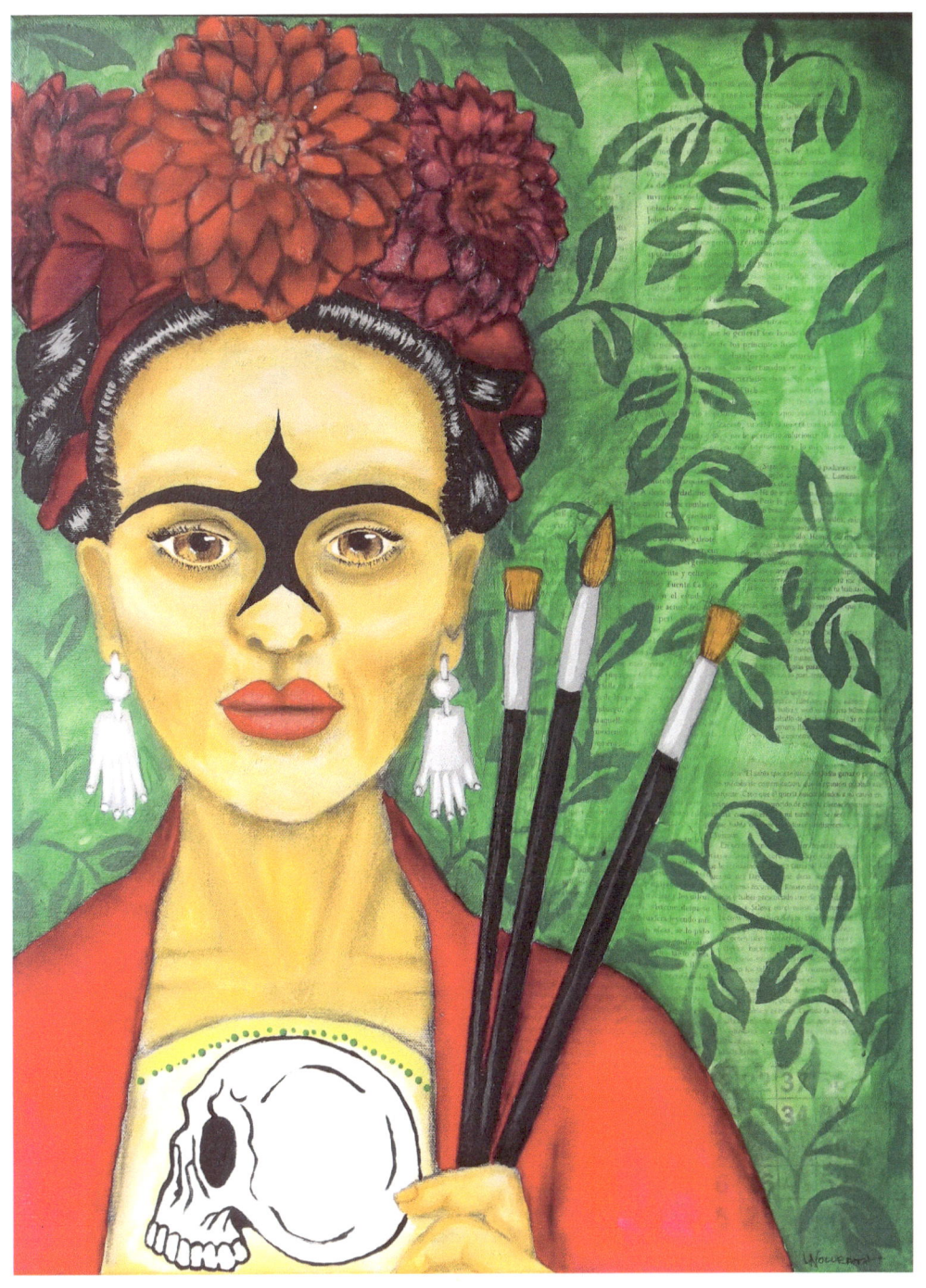

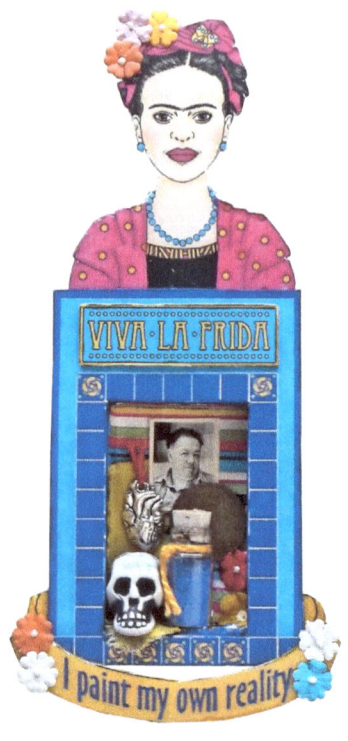
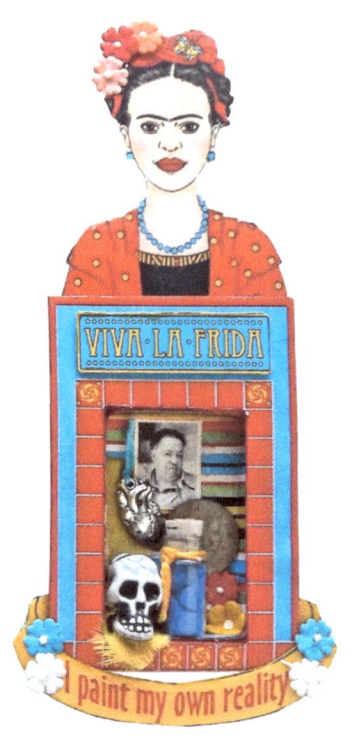

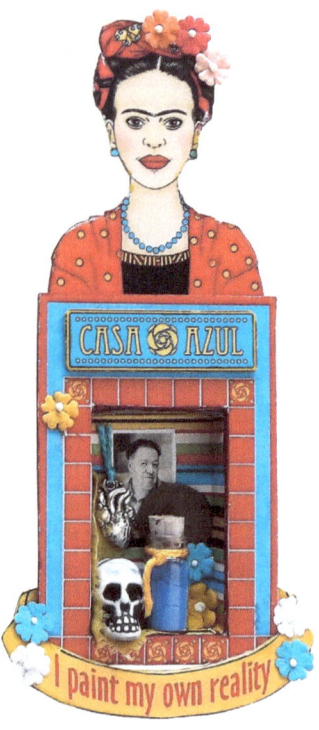
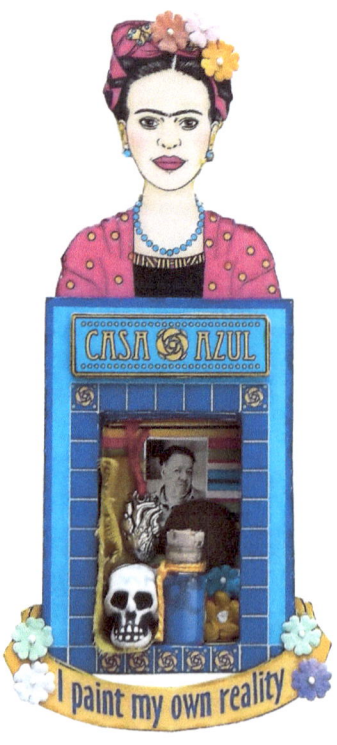

Left: *Set Frida Matchbox Shrines*
Color laser prints, chipboard, acrylics and found objects.

Right: *Set of Frida Altoids Tin Shrines*
Metal Altoids tins, color laser prints, and found objects.

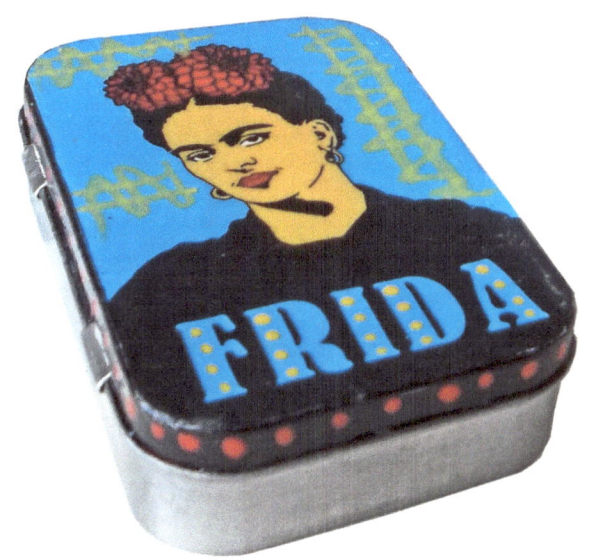

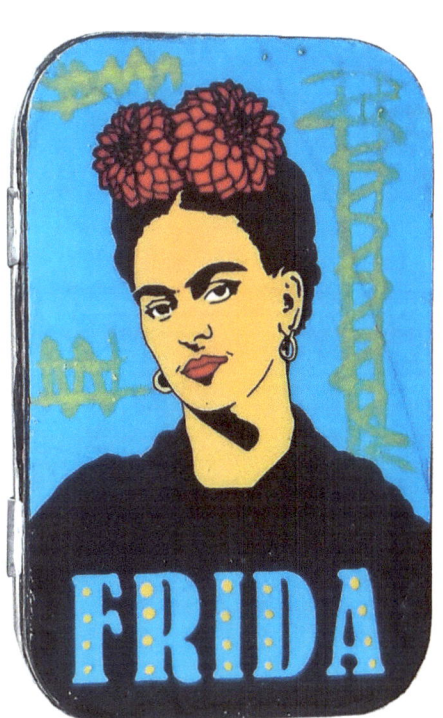

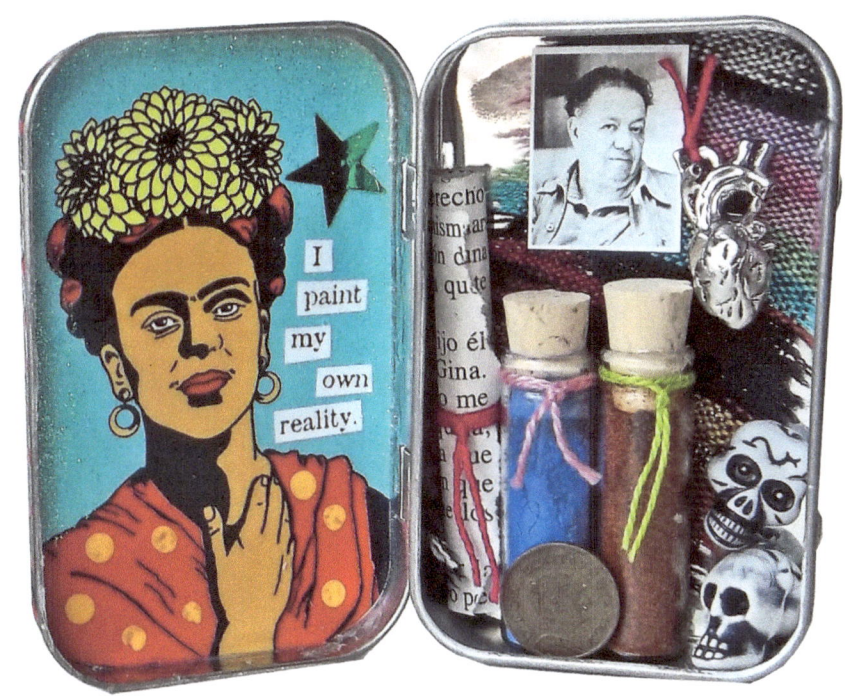

Amy Jo Garner

Del City, Oklahoma

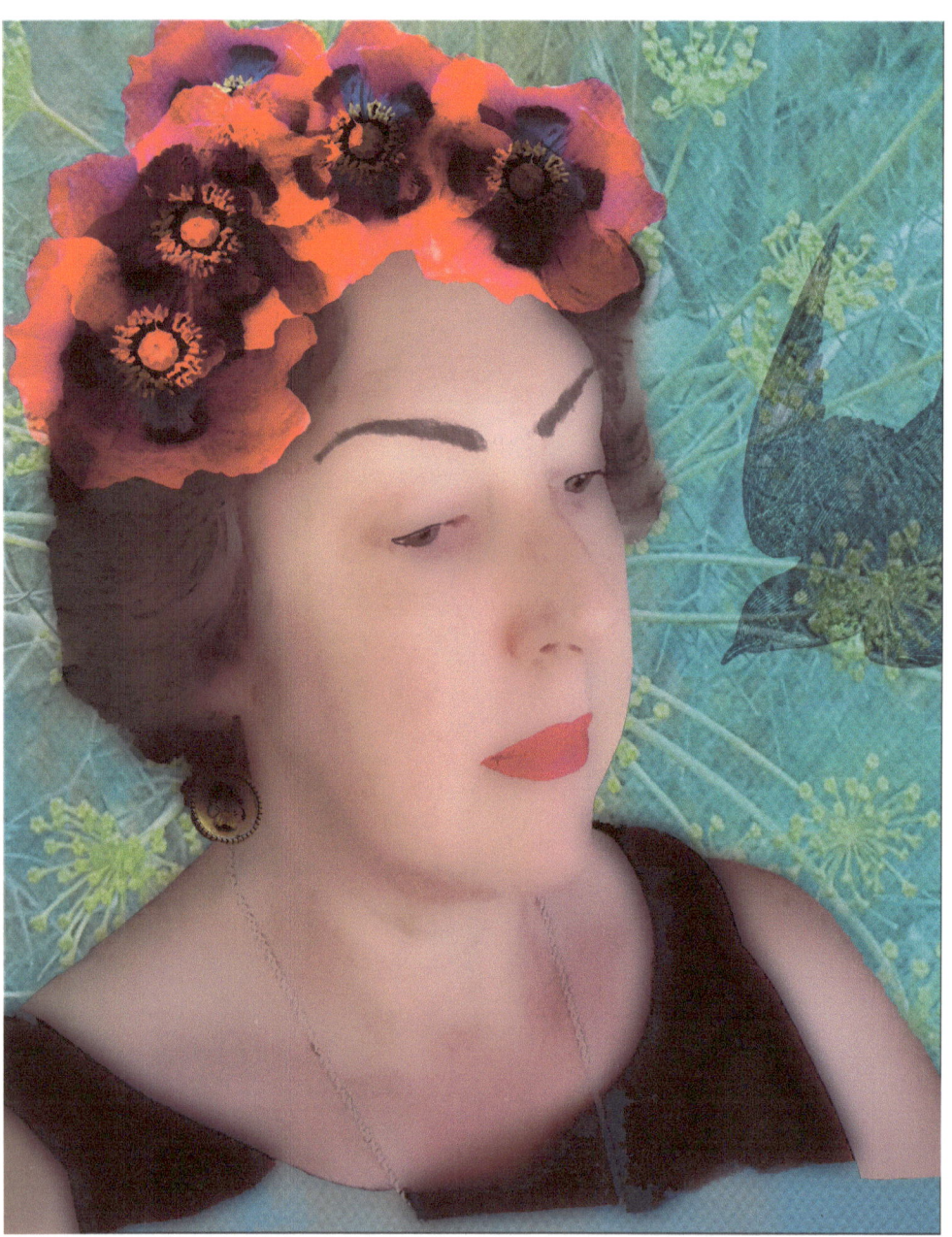

Here's what Amy had to say about Frida:

"Frida's self portraiture using natural elements and animals has always inspired me. Her willingness to present and paint herself as she wished to be seen inspires me to create art that reflects me and my connection to the natural world. This Frida-inspired self portrait features photos of poppies and dill from my garden, a resin and viola pendent I crafted, and a shadow of a purple martin."

2016 Self Portrait Frida-Style
Digital collage printed with archival ink on 8 x 10 inch matte photo paper.

More of Amy's work can be seen on her Instagram account, amyjogarner.

Terry Dee Yackley

Shelley, Idaho

Here's what Terry had to say about Frida:

"Two things about Frida always inspired me. First, she bore great pain with strength. Second, she allowed photographers to capture her image. She became comfortable with her own face.

And then, she was also alone. I've been alone much of the time lately. At first, I felt abandoned! But several years into living alone, I find myself centered there. Since many of Frida's works were based on her constantly available model - herself - I decided to LOOK at me, myself, and paint a self-portrait."

Self-Portrait a la Frida
Acrylic on 18 x 24 inch canvas board.

More of Terry's work can be seen on her Facebook page, Burning Need.

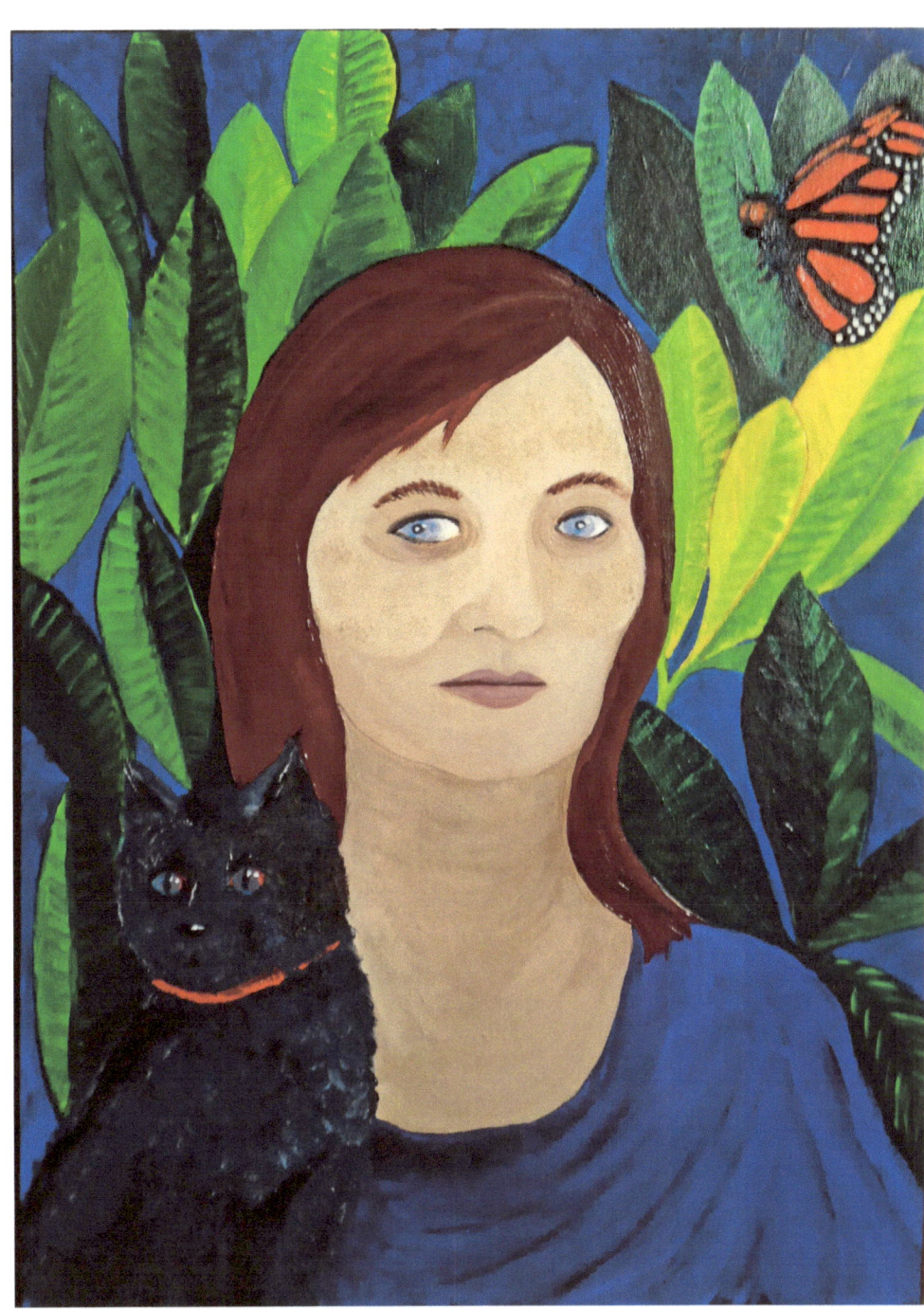

Blanca Perez

Dallas, Texas

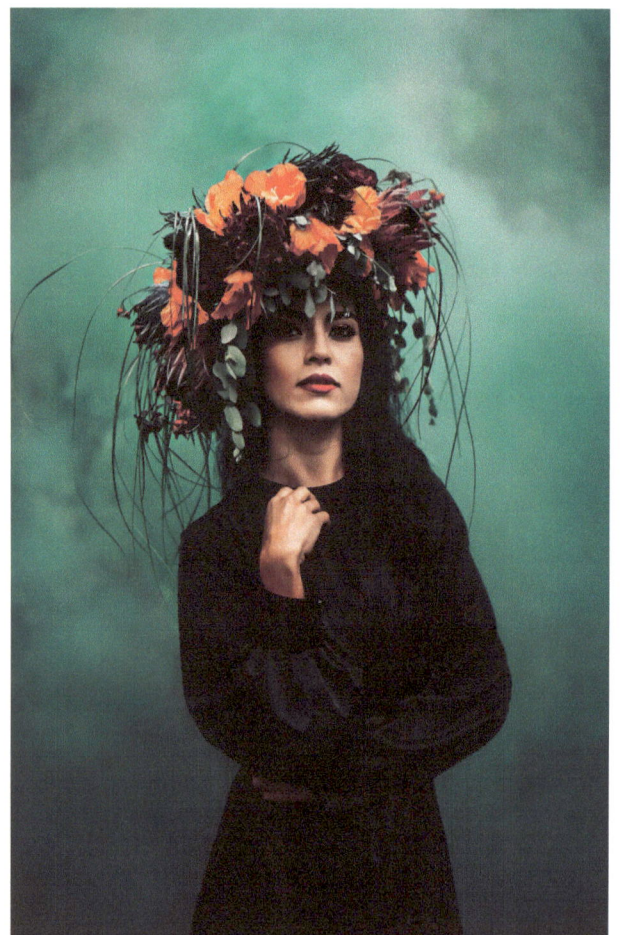
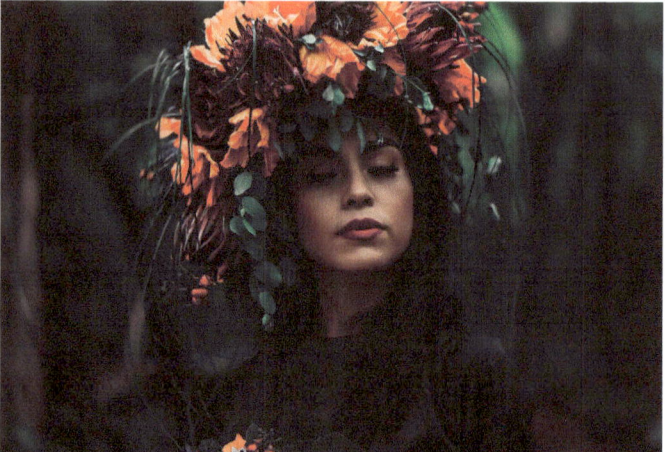
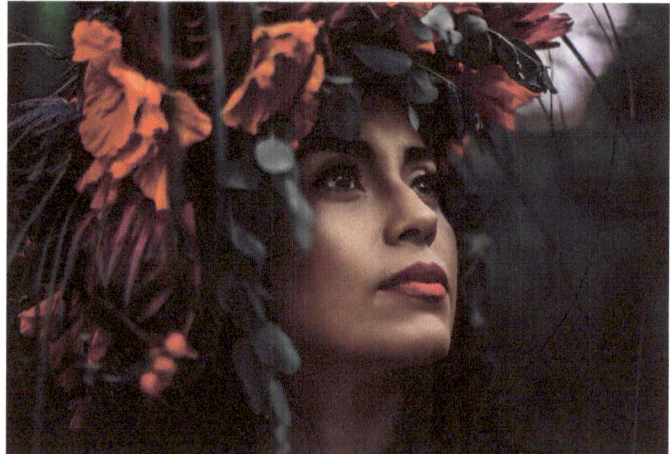

Essence
Model: Elisa Carreon
Florist: Sonia Muñoz-Ponce/Gardenia-Dallas

Here's what Blanca had to say about Frida:

"I am inspired by Frida's strength and courage to be bold. To hurt openly and embrace her essence to the core. She found comfort and inspiration in her pain. "

More of Blanca's work can be seen on web site, blancaeperez.com.

Lulu Moonwood Murakami

Portland, Oregon

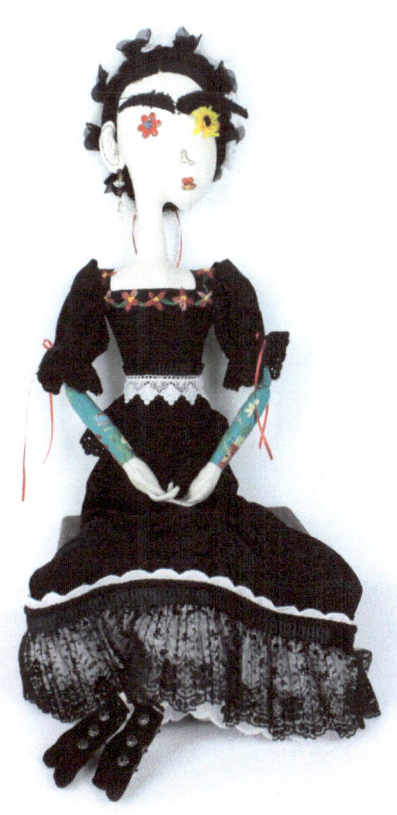

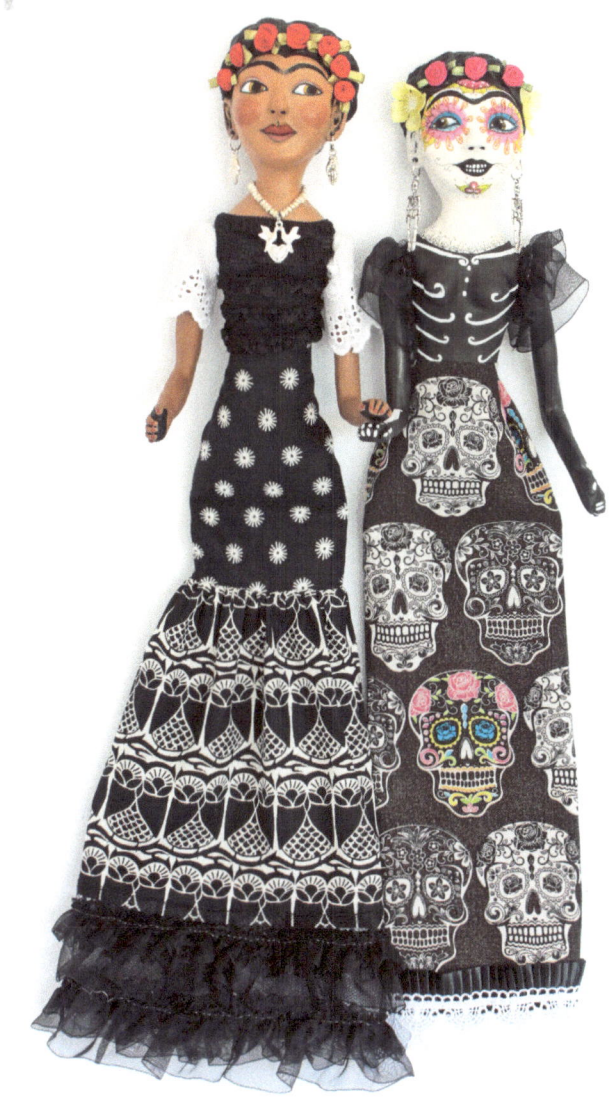

Above: *Frida Solita*
Cloth doll. 41 inches tall.

Right: *Frida Hoy y Mañana*
Cloth doll. 21 inches tall.

Here's what Lulu had to say about Frida:

"Frida has always inspired me for her inner strength, determination, and self-awareness. She draws us into her inner world, allowing us to feel what she feels."

More of Allegra's work can be seen on web site, lulumoonart.com.

Inspired by Frida Postcard Swap

In conjunction with this issue, I hosted a Frida-themed postcard swap. These are some of the handmade, 4 x 6 inch postcards submitted for the swap, quotes from their creators, and quotes from Frida herself.

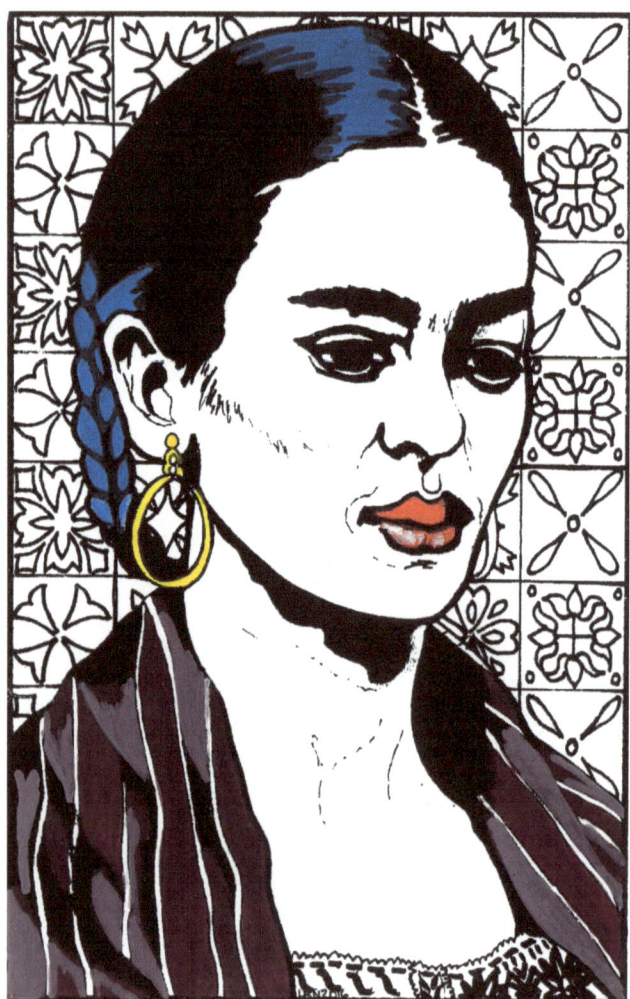

Lori Rael Leslie-Northon
Albuquerque, New Mexico

"I am inspired by Frida's emotional outpouring in her artwork, and by her determination."

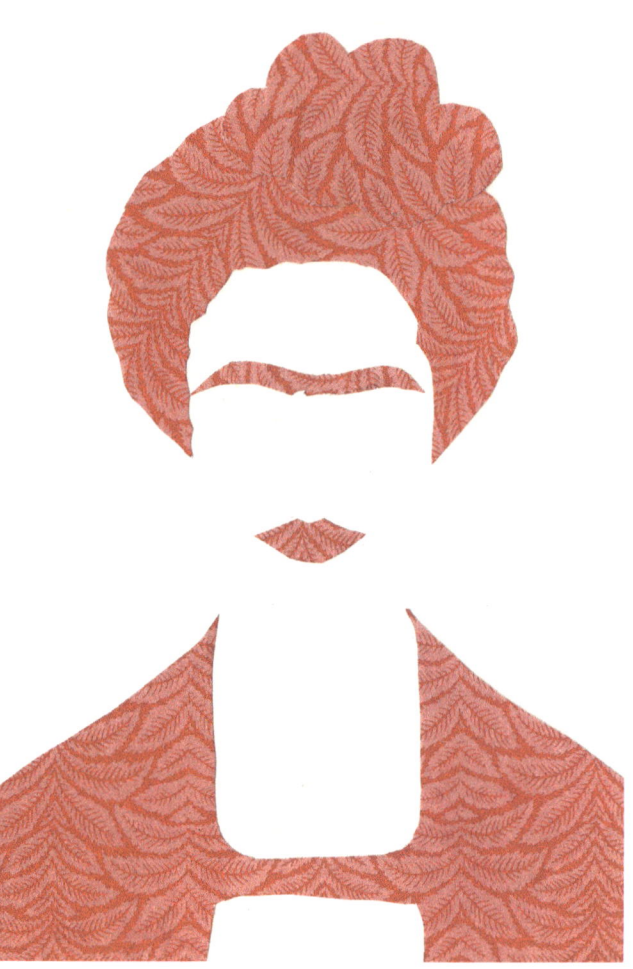

L.A. Smith-Buxton
Bothell, Washington

"I am inspired by Frida's unwillingness to be categorized or easily defined.."

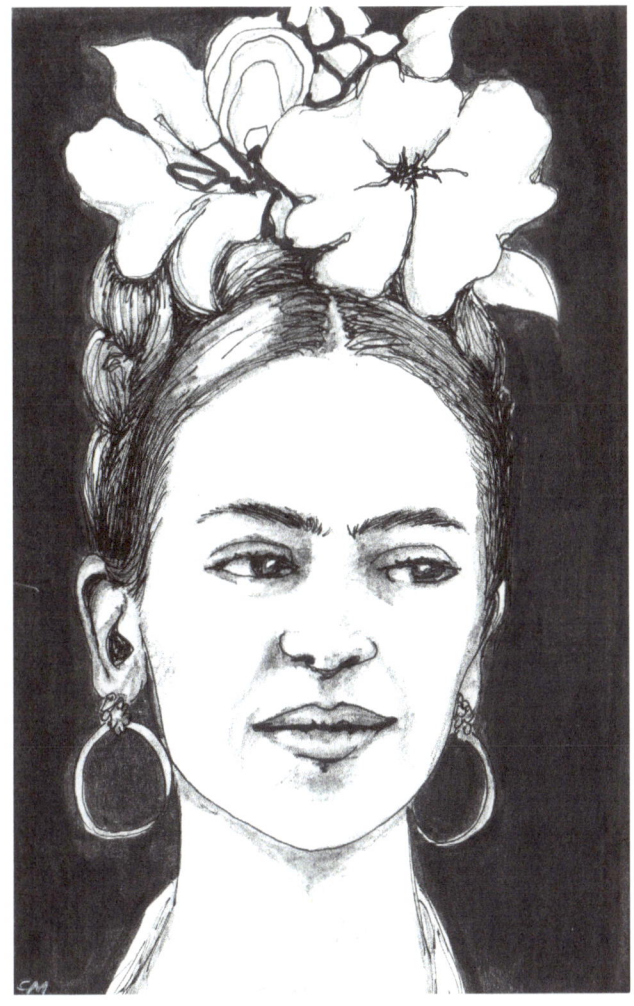

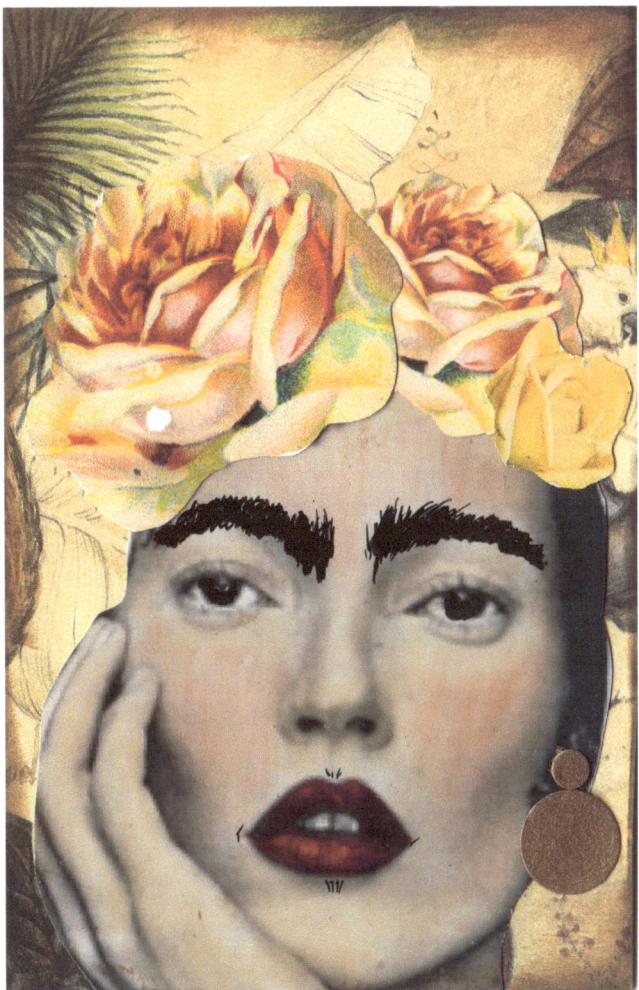

Carolyn Myles
Smyrna, Georgie

Esta Berman-Price
Stamford, Connecticut

"I am inspired by Frida's tenacity; she never gave up. Her acceptance of her life; she didn't want pity. Her beautiful art; she expressed her deepest emotions and communicated through her paintings."

"I am inspired by Frida's determination to work through debilitating pain to paint her artistic journey."

**"Nothing is worth more than laughter.
It is strength to laugh and to abandon oneself, to be light.
Tragedy is the most ridiculous thing."**

> "My painting carries with it the message of pain."

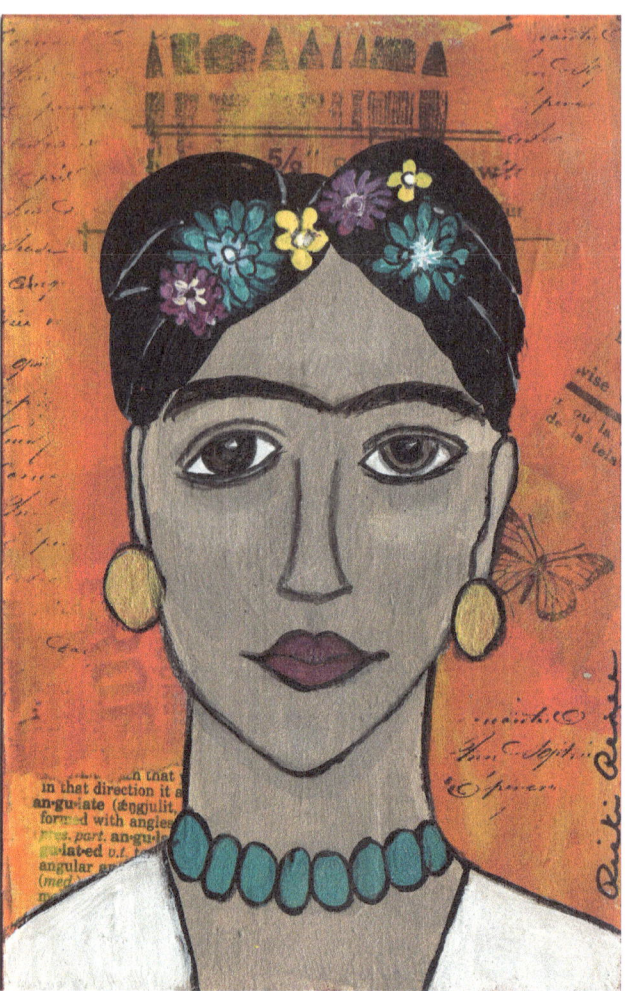

Ricki Midbrod
Tucson, Arizona

"I am inspired by Frida's perseverance to create. She had every excuse to quit, but she never did."

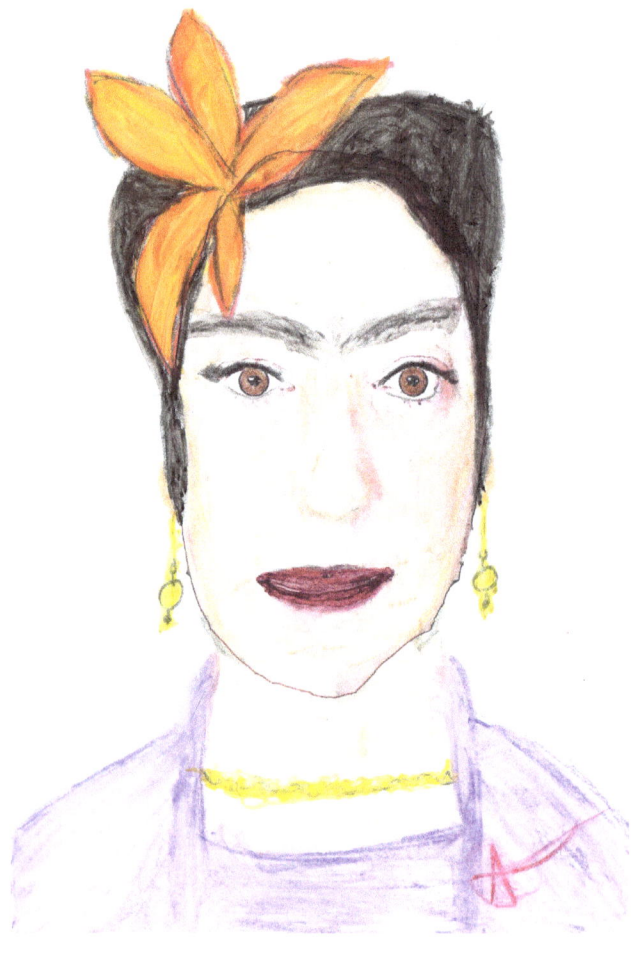

Amy Jo Garner
Del City, Oklahoma

"I am inspired by Frida's persistence and dedication to her art, despite a troubling marriage, miscarriages, and illnesses."

> "I paint self-portraits because I am so often alone, because I am the person I know best."

> **"I am not sick. I am broken.**
> **But I am happy to be alive as long as I can paint."**

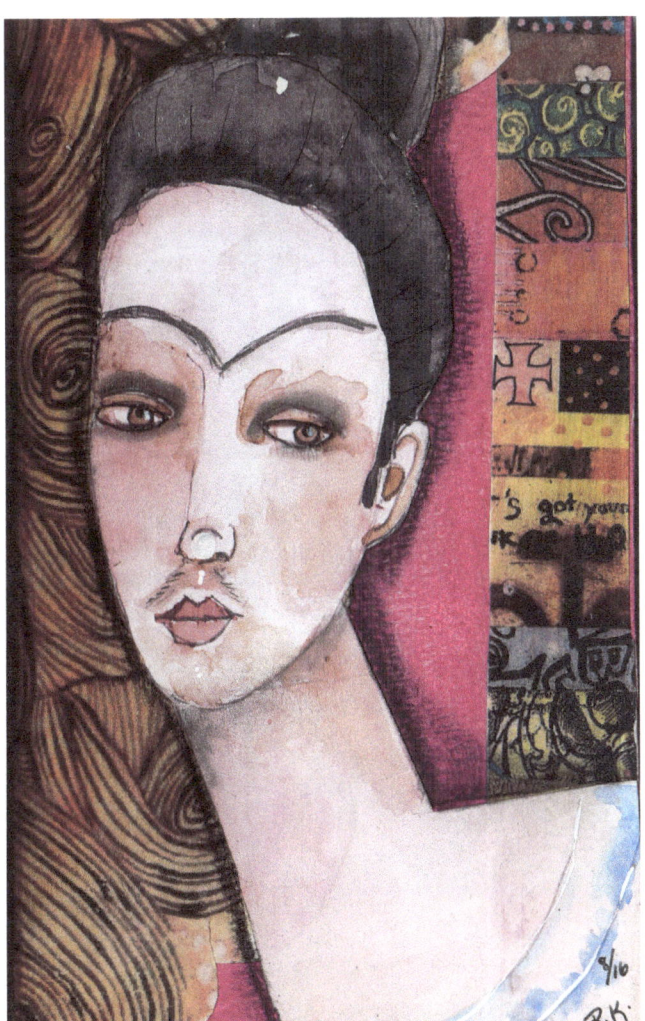 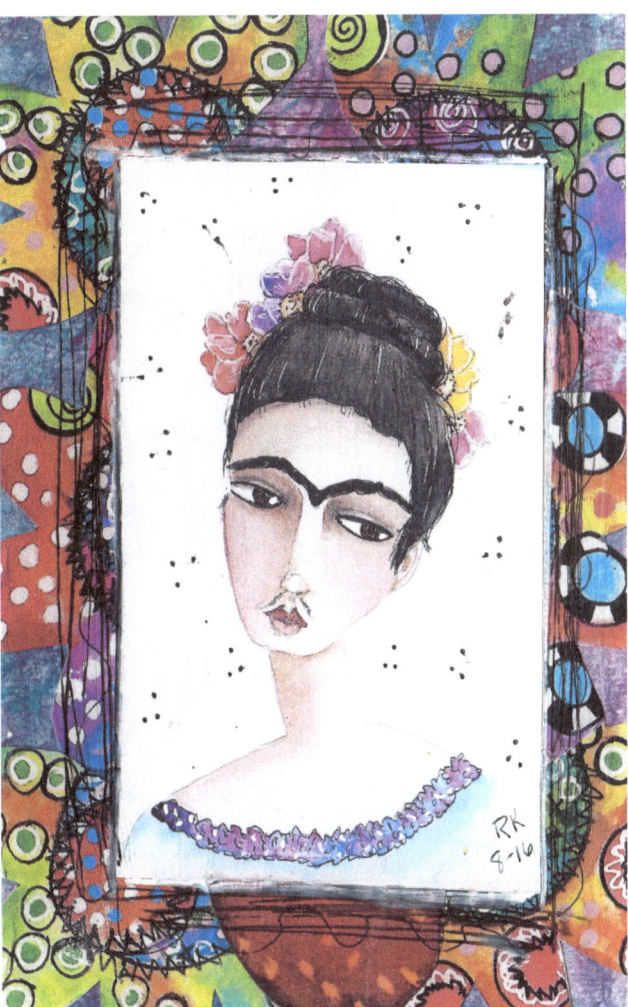

Robin Krieger
Kenbridge, Virginia

"Frida's art inspires me to use my feelings in my paintings. I'm now in kidney failure, and when I first started I kept a journal to help me deal with all the feelings that went with that life changing event. It helped me so much, and it was Frida who inspired a lot of that art. I have been on dialysis for over a year, and am on my sixth journal. Frida was and is my biggest inspiration."

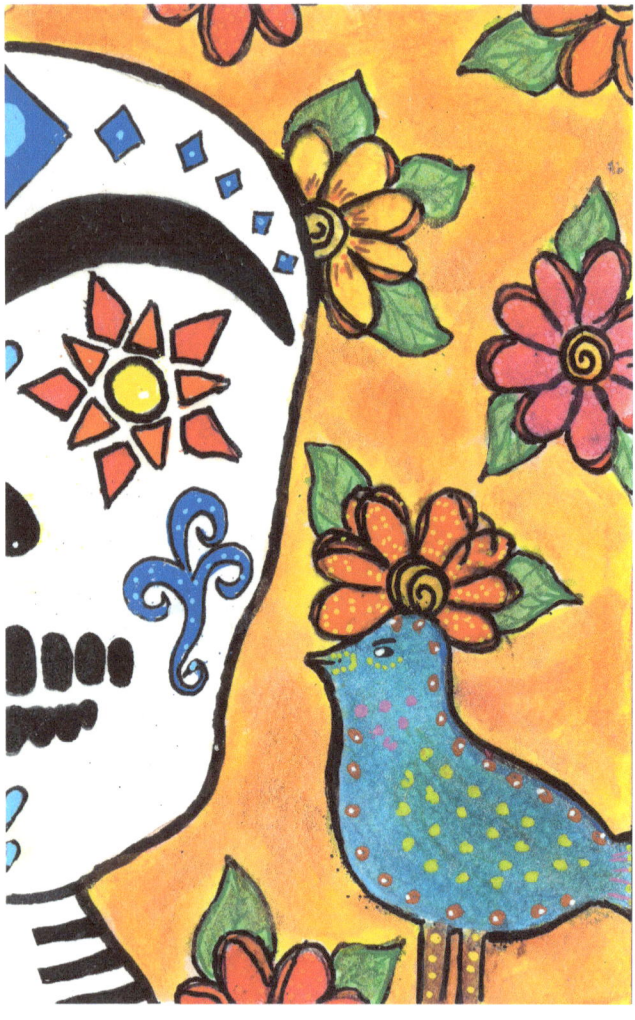

Mary Ann Gross
Memphis, Tennessee

"I am inspired by Mexican art and culture. Frida expresses both use of color, and provides examples of her culture. She had a hard life, but let her are pull her through many hurdles."

"I don't paint dreams
or nightmares,
I paint my own reality."

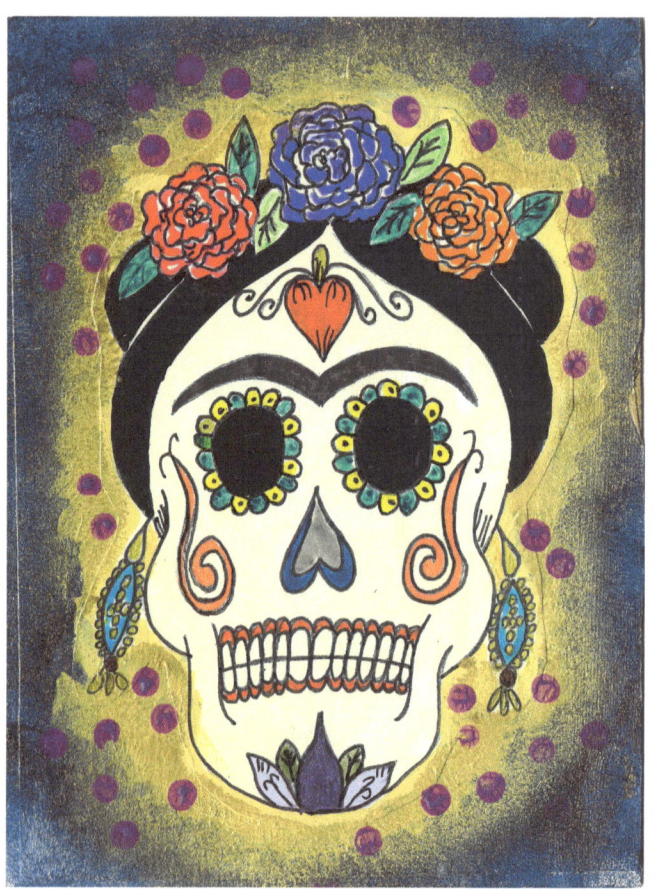

K.P. Berg
Tubac, Arizona

"I am inspired by Frida's colors, her tenacity, her individuality, and her style."

"I drank to drown my sorrows,
but the damned things learned how to swim."

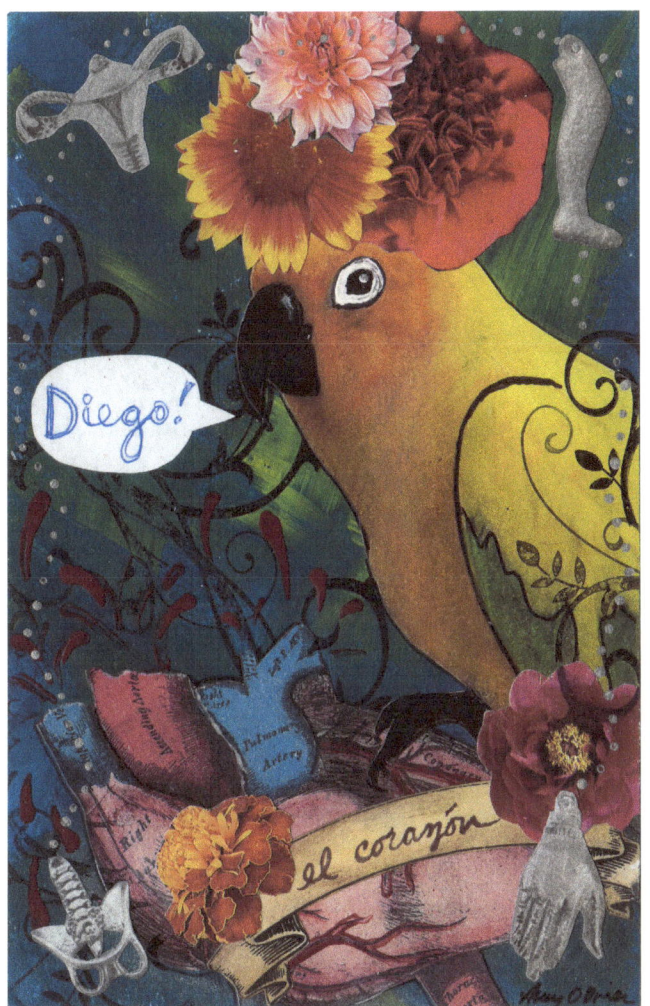

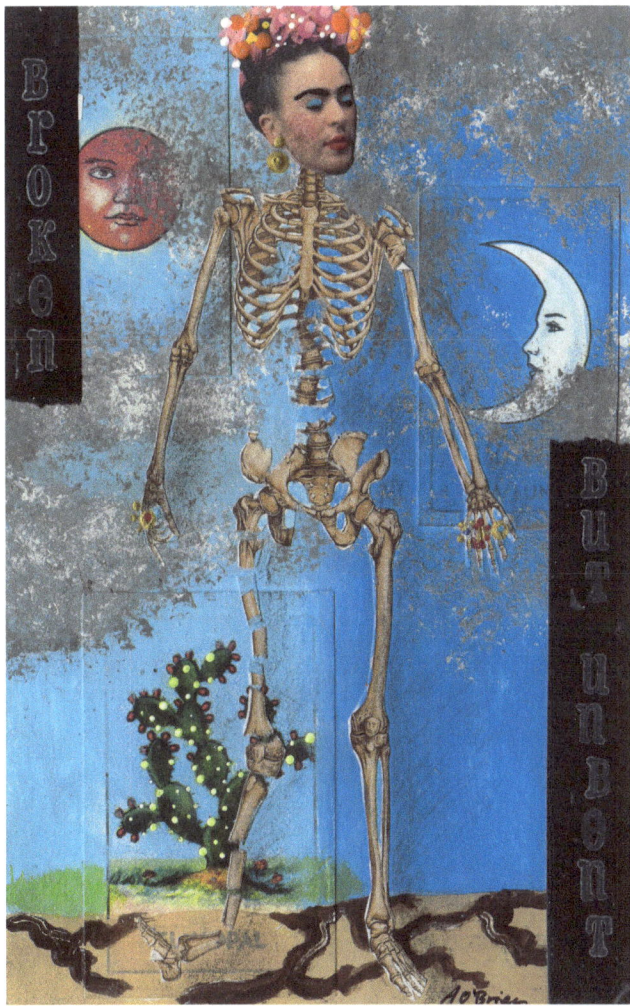

Amy O'Brien
Santa Clarita,
California

"I am inspired by Frida's ability to visually depict her pain and work through her emotions in her art. Her raw honesty creates an instant connection with the viewer."

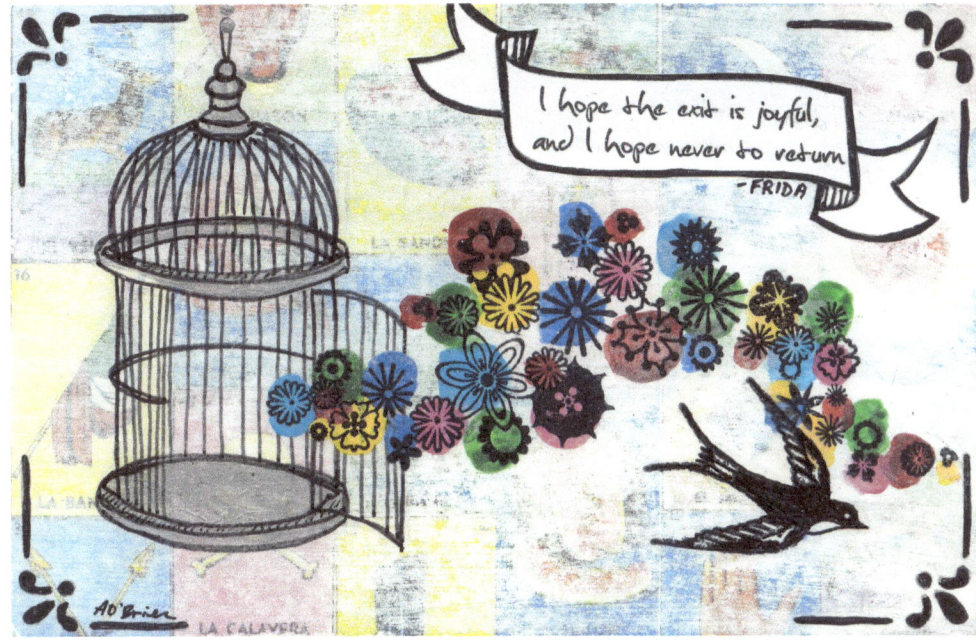

"There have been two great accidents in my life.
One was the trolley, and the other was Diego.
Diego was by far the worst."

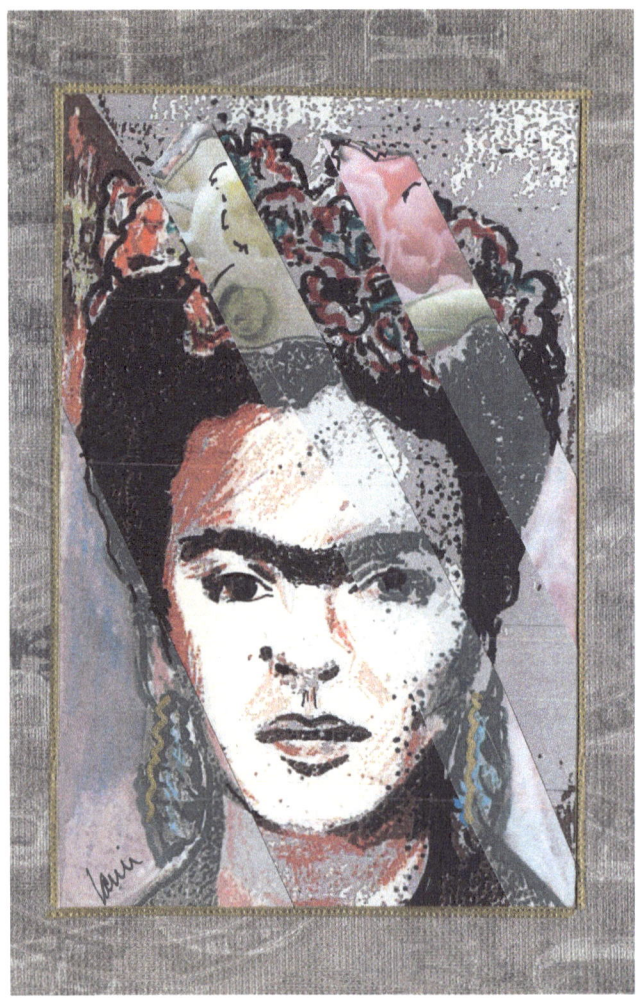
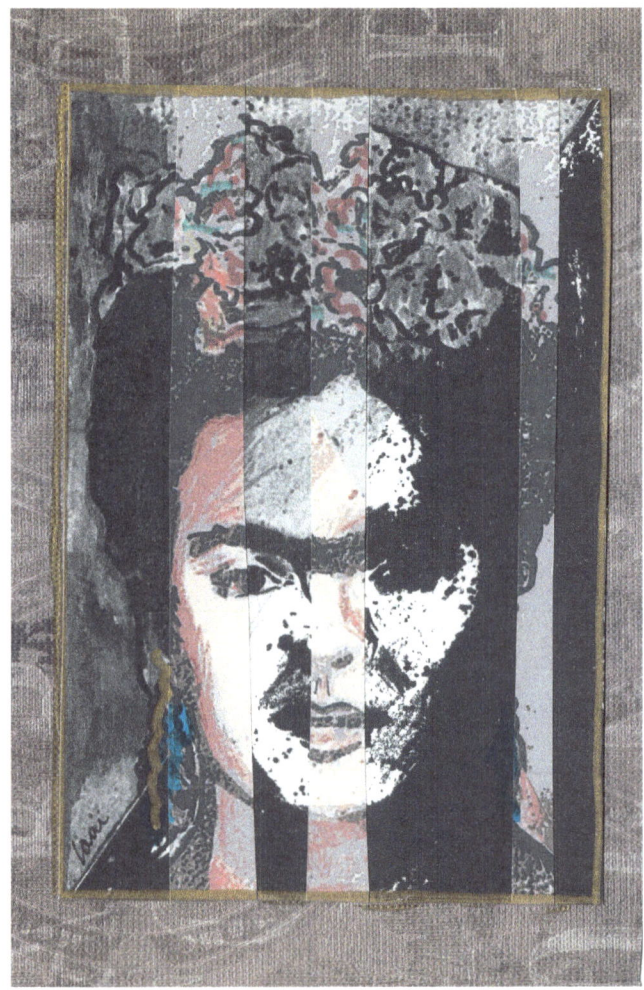

Lani Kyea
Clayton, New Mexico

"I am inspired by Frida's embracing beauty and a full life through the pain. Her love of viva la vida."

www.ingramcontent.com/pod-product-compliance
Lightning Source LLC
Chambersburg PA
CBHW050428180526
45159CB00005B/2452